MW00698649

Out of the **MOUTHS** of **BABES**... and **DUDES**

quotations collected by
JOHN BYTHEWAY

Library of Congress Cataloging-in-Publication Data

Out of the mouths of babes . . . and dudes/compiled by John Bytheway.
    p. cm.
    ISBN 1-57345-241-6

    1. Mormon Youth—Religious life—Quotations. 2. Spiritual life—Mormon Church—Quotations, maxims, etc. 3. Church of Jesus Christ of Latter-day Saints—Quotations, maxims, etc. 4. Mormon Church—Quotations, maxims, etc. I. Bytheway, John, 1962–   .
BX8643.Y6098   1997
289.3′32′0835—dc21   97-14590
                                                    CIP

Printed in Mexico
10 9 8 7 6 5 4 3 2 1

For years, I've been keeping a list of interesting things I've heard Latter-day Saint teenagers say, mostly at youth conference testimony meetings. The list sat in the back of my planner for a long time, not doing anybody any good. One day, I shared it with my friend Brad Wilcox, and he added several of his own favorite teenager quotes. All together, they make quite a collection! Some of them are profound, some are insightful, and some are hilarious. We think you might enjoy them too. You'll find out that many other LDS youth feel just like you do—about the gospel, about the embarrassing way their brother acts at stake dances, and about keeping their standards high when they're with their friends. So here they are: my favorite quotes from "out of the mouths of babes . . . and dudes."

At first, when I heard we were having
a testimony meeting, I thought,
"Oh great, we get to go watch a bunch of
women cry, and a bunch of
men talk about themselves."

A young man

It's typical for the girls to cry,

but I love it when the boys cry.

A young woman

I've never had a problem with the Word of Wisdom, I'm morally clean, my parents are still happily married . . . I guess what I mean is that this conference didn't bring a total turnaround in my life, but it has given me the confidence in my own spirituality to keep on living the gospel and keeping the commandments.

A young woman

I'm standing here because
I want to bear my testimony, and
there's a girl out there I want to impress.

A young man

I don't have a testimony of everything,
but I have a testimony of enough.

A young man

I know that it's very important
to share your testimony,
because if you don't, it weakens.

A young man

Seminary gives us the knowledge
and youth conference makes it explode.

A young man

I'm afraid to go home because
what I've learned is not welcome there.
Let your friends know
what your church is all about—
to keep it to yourself should be a crime.

A non-LDS young woman

Celestial Kingdom =
Eternal Youth Conference.

A young man

I think the Spirit just put a sleeping bag in the back and has been here the whole time.

A young man

Either I feel the Spirit or

I'm gonna be sick.

A young man

I used to rely on my parents' testimony,

but I needed to get my own.

I don't want to be good for nothin'.

A young man

I don't think we realize how lucky we are.
I have a lot of friends at school
who are very confused. I feel so lucky,
because I know who I am,
and I know where I'm going.

A young man

When people tease you about the Church,
they're really just curious.

A young woman

I was coming home from a football game, and the group I was riding with pulled out some beer. They started to pass a can of beer around, taking sips or drinks. When it got to me I just calmly threw it out the window. They were shocked, but then they all decided that they didn't need it and threw the rest out the window.

A young man

We're Mormons, but we really do have fun.
We don't drink and use drugs,
but we have great parties.
We can have fun with a bag of Doritos
and a Twister game.

A young man

When I first met him, every other word was a cuss word. He noticed that I never cussed no matter what happened. So he decided to stop. Pretty soon he was asking me a whole bunch of questions about the Church. I guess I answered them right, because then he asked if he could have a Book of Mormon. I wrote my testimony in it and gave it to him. I never knew how much a little missionary work could build your own testimony.

A young woman

It's hard for me to always know the right
thing to say or do to touch someone's heart.
Sometimes I'd just like to say,
"Hey! The gospel's true!
I wouldn't lie to you!"

A young woman

Read the Book of Mormon even if you
don't get all the thee's and thou's.
If it's wrong, God will let you know.
But I think you'll be surprised.

A young woman to her non-LDS friend

I'm so thankful for missionaries.
I hope not only will missionaries do their
work but that everyone will!
I know how happy I've been
since I introduced Jamie to the Church.
She knows it is true, and I hope someday my
parents will see the light of the Church too.

A young woman

There's not a day or night where I don't
wish and hope this world will come to know
the joy that I have because of the Church.

A young woman

It is the prettiest feeling
to have your friend baptized.

A young woman

My parents were only gonna have two kids

. . . then the missionaries came . . .

now there's nine of us.

A young man

If I would've known I was going to spend the next two weeks with my brother Mike, I would've taken the next plane to Siberia.

Brother to brother

I'd like to tell my brother that I love him,
even though sometimes
I act like I don't know him.
If you saw him at a dance,
you'd know why.

Sister to brother

I wish my sister could see how ugly her boyfriends are . . .

Brother to sister

I want my sister to know that I love her, and my brother to know that I like him.

A young woman

My sister is such an example
of total honesty. The other day
she got an extra chicken nugget in her lunch
and took it back.

A young woman

My dad is so outgoing
it's embarrassing to me sometimes.

 บ๊ะ

A young woman

Prayer is easy to stop and
so hard to start again—
but operators are standing by.

A young woman

When you pray, you should ask for help,

not tell him what to do,

'cause He's in charge.

A young man

Heavenly Father is so much smarter than us,
so we should take his advice.

A young man

The Holy Ghost can't steer a parked car.
You have to be moving to have him help you.

A young man

I learned that prayers to Heavenly Father
are usually answered
through another person.

A young woman

Anyone that's not friends
with those in your ward, that's wrong.
You should be friends,
that's the way Zion should be.

A young woman

I got a phone call from a girl I got into a fight with. She told me she missed me today. She wanted to know how I was and if she'd see me tomorrow. Earlier my best friend called me and said she missed me too. Then my seminary teacher called and said she missed me. You don't know the love I felt. I felt so good about myself. I thought, "People really do care about me!"

A young woman

Sometimes the people
in the Church can be mean,
but the gospel can never hurt you;
the gospel is what you can lean on.

A young woman

There's one person who will never fail me—
that's my Savior.

A young woman

A couple of those drops of blood
were for me.

A young woman

I am a nerd; I'm proud to admit it.
I've seen both sides of the hill,
being popular and being a nerd.
I'd rather be a nerd—nerds have to dare to
stand up for what they believe.
So I challenge you all to be a nerd.

A young man

Earlier she had made fun of me

for being a Mormon.

Now she was saying,

"I wish I was like you.

You'll be worthy to wear white

at your wedding; please don't change."

A young woman

I miss the days when I was good.

A young woman

Being good isn't easy.

It's so easy to be bad.

A young woman

I used to always have my rock music
playing and then my tape player broke.
I went crazy until I realized that now
I could listen to the Spirit–
before I could never hear him.

A young man

Those who watch R-rated movies

are just paying Satan for lessons.

A young man

I just wish that I won't forget
what I had to go through to be forgiven.
I'm afraid I might decide
I liked my rebellious life better
and go back to being an idiot.

A young woman

I'm starting to regain my testimony
of the Church. I hope that through all of the
hard trials I've experienced
I may be able to influence others
to steer clear of sin. It is not a happy path.
It may seem fun, but one mistake
leads to others, and it's just a slippery slide
that ends in the mud.

A young woman

God allows "U" turns.

A young man

I'm really excited about life.
I have almost my whole life to live,
and I can make it good or bad.
It is comforting to know that Heavenly Father
is there for me when I make good or bad
choices, even before I make a choice.

A young woman

I'm glad I'm not perfect,

'cause then I wouldn't be able to grow.

A young woman

If you don't have fun the right way,
you won't have fun after you're dead.

A young man

I had one of those moments
when every lesson I've ever been taught
comes together and they scream,
"We told you! We told you if you did this
you'd be happy! We told you if you kept the
commandments you'd be at peace!
We told you the scriptures
hold the answers to your problems!
We told you, we told you!"

A young woman

I used to think my life was horrible.

But compared to you guys,

my life is perfect.

A young man

To the Mormons in my school I say,

"It's okay, we can do this,

we can be strong."

A young woman

The way we live is worth it,

just to feel this way.

XOX

A young woman

If you don't have an open heart,
you'll never have an open mind.

A young woman

I can't be proud of many things.

I'm not the prettiest girl,

and I'm not the smartest girl.

But I know that my Savior is Jesus Christ.

A young woman

Don't let your problems get you down—
unless it gets you down on your knees.

A young woman

I know we're supposed to clean up the
world before Jesus comes,
and that'll be hard because
I can't even keep my room clean.

A young woman

I love to hold my scriptures,
'cause I can't be with Christ right now,
so I'll just hold these.

A young woman

Prayer is like our telephone to reach

Heavenly Father and Jesus.

A young man

I used to be afraid
of Christ's Second Coming.
I don't know why I used to be afraid.
I probably just didn't understand.
All I know now is that I can hardly wait!

A young woman

I love my Savior.
There is so much more
I need to learn about Him,
but I know now that He lives.

A young man

Probably the most wonderful thing

about this youth conference for me

is that for the first time I truly realized

that I was not alone. There really are other

kids like me who want

so desperately to live the gospel.

A young woman

It's kinda weird that for some reason
we all came here and are in the same ward.
In our group there are peer pressures,
but a good kind. A kind that says,
"do good," "get prepared," and
"be what God knows you can be."

A young man

We have lots of Mormon parties,
and if you hear about one, you're invited . . .
if you bring food.

A young man

I look forward to the time

when we meet again whether in this world

or the next because

we can be together forever someday.

The righteous need never say good-bye.

A young man

I've done a lot of thinking lately,
and I've decided to give in to the Church.
I guess I kind of thought I was too normal,
but y'know what? I'm *not* normal,
and I *love* the Church of Jesus Christ!
I want to marry a returned missionary!
I want to have lots of kids!
I want to sing "Jesus Wants Me for a Sunbeam"
and say "beam" really obnoxious with my kids!

A young woman

The Church is true . . .

that's my basic overall attitude.

A young woman

Lately, I have been so appreciative
of the gospel and can feel
Heavenly Father's love for me.
It's as if someone has just
turned on a light and I can see clearly!
I know that this church is true,
otherwise I don't think I'd bother with all the
work involved in living its teachings!

A young woman

I never get letters from people I look up to.
I usually get letters from
the Wells Fargo Bank telling me they've
added $.06 to my account.

A young woman

God has always been by my side,
but I didn't reach up to take his hand.
I'm hanging on for dear life now!

A young woman

Kissing takes on a whole new perspective

when I think that my future wife

might be saving her perfect kiss just for me.

I want to marry a girl who

hasn't kissed a lot of guys,

and I'm sure she wants the same for me.

A young man

When God opens a door for me,

I will make sure I'm ready,

and I will be through that door in a flash.

A young woman

Kissing takes on a whole new perspective

when I think that my future wife

might be saving her perfect kiss just for me.

I want to marry a girl who

hasn't kissed a lot of guys,

and I'm sure she wants the same for me.

A young man

When God opens a door for me,

I will make sure I'm ready,

and I will be through that door in a flash.

⚡

A young woman

You guys, don't ever
compare yourself to others.
I'll forgive you this one time,
but don't let it happen again, understood?
Lecture over, you may be seated.

A young woman

I can't wait till school's out,
only four more weeks! Early-morning
seminary will be out in two weeks!
Joy! I won't have to sleep in my classes,
so maybe I'll learn something
the last two weeks of school.

A young woman

My friend was at a dance in July, and he was checking out everyone who had a CTR ring. He said so many people were wearing them that it wasn't just a warm fuzzy, it was a hot fuzzy!

A young woman

I've been having a great day,
and I'm in the mood to tell everyone how
great they all are. You might be thinking,
"Who spiked her Sprite?" But I'm just really
happy and I thought I might inform you.

A young woman

Boy, it's great what the Holy Ghost can do, but it's not great if you don't listen.

A young woman

Yesterday I baby-sat a two-week-old baby.

I love babies.

I want some when I become a mother.

A young woman

The first thing my friend noticed about the Church was the basketball hoop in the cultural hall. I noticed the Spirit right inside the front door.

A young man

They say the Spirit feels like a burning.
Well, then call the fire station
because there is a blaze here
that is out of control.

A young man

I need a calculator to keep track of how often I count on the Savior.

A young man

Prayers are the one thing that never come back stamped, "Return to Sender."

A young woman

If man came from the dust
and will return to the dust, then there is
someone under my brother's bed who is
either coming or going.

A young man

The new kid in school was named
Nephi Fielding Pratt.
I figured he had to be a Mormon.

A young man

Life is like a wrestling match. The coaches have taught us all we need to know. It's up to us now to go out there and pin Satan.

A young man

I'm a lifeguard during the week and an eternal lifeguard on Sunday.

A young man

I'm always happy
'cause I don't see no use
in bein' sad.

A young man

From what I can tell
from my brother's letters,
the Spirit must live at the MTC
and just visit everywhere else.

A young man

A lot of girls in the stake don't like to dance with the 14-year-old boys because they are too young, but my motto is, "Train up a 14-year-old in the way he should go, and when he is 16 he will not depart from it."

A young woman

I always wondered how people could say, "I love you" to people they don't even know, but now I realize that we all knew each other well a long time before. We're really just finally meeting up with old friends.

A young woman